Key Facts™ on

Lebanon

~*Essential Information on Lebanon*~

By Patrick W. Nee

The Internationalist®
www.internationalist.com

The Internationalist®

International Business, Investment, and Travel

Published by:

The Internationalist Publishing Company

96 Walter Street/ Suite 200

Boston, MA 02131, USA

Tel: 617-354-7722

www.internationalist.com

PN@internationalist.com

Table Of Contents

Chapter 1: Background

Chapter 2: Geography

Chapter 3: People and Society

Chapter 4: Government and Key Leaders

Chapter 5: Economy

Chapter 6: Energy

Chapter 7: Communications

Chapter 8: Transportation

Chapter 9: Military

Chapter 10: Transnational Issues

Map of Lebanon

Chapter 1: Background

Following World War I, France acquired a mandate over the northern portion of the former Ottoman Empire province of Syria. The French demarcated the region of Lebanon in 1920 and granted this area independence in 1943. Since independence the country has been marked by periods of political turmoil interspersed with prosperity built on its position as a regional center for finance and trade. The country's 1975-90 civil war that resulted in an estimated 120,000 fatalities, was followed by years of social and political instability. Sectarianism is a key element of Lebanese political life. Neighboring Syria has long influenced Lebanon's foreign policy and internal policies, and its military occupied Lebanon from 1976 until 2005. The Lebanon-based Hizballah militia and Israel continued attacks and counterattacks against each other after Syria's withdrawal, and fought a brief war in 2006. Lebanon's borders with Syria and Israel remain unresolved.

Chapter 2: Geography

Location:

Middle East, bordering the Mediterranean Sea,
between Israel and Syria

Geographic coordinates:

33 50 N, 35 50 E

Map references:

Middle East

Area:

total: 10,400 sq km

country comparison to the world: 170

land: 10,230 sq km

water: 170 sq km

Area - comparative:

about 0.7 times the size of Connecticut

Land boundaries:

total: 454 km

border countries: Israel 79 km, Syria 375 km

Coastline:

225 km

Maritime claims:

territorial sea: 12 nm

Climate:

Mediterranean; mild to cool, wet winters with hot, dry summers; Lebanon mountains experience heavy winter snows

Terrain:

narrow coastal plain; El Beqaa (Bekaa Valley) separates Lebanon and Anti-Lebanon Mountains

Elevation extremes:

lowest point: Mediterranean Sea 0 m

highest point: Qornet es Saouda 3,088 m

Natural resources:

limestone, iron ore, salt, water-surplus state in a water-deficit region, arable land

Land use:

arable land: 10.72%

permanent crops: 12.06%

other: 77.22% (2011)

Irrigated land:

1,040 sq km (2003)

Total renewable water resources:

4.5 cu km (2011)

Freshwater withdrawal (domestic/industrial/agricultural):

total: 1.31 cu km/yr (29%/11%/60%)

per capita: 316.8 cu m/yr (2005)

Natural hazards:

dust storms, sandstorms

Environment - current issues:

deforestation; soil erosion; desertification; air pollution in Beirut from vehicular traffic and the burning of industrial wastes; pollution of coastal waters from raw sewage and oil spills

Environment - international agreements:

party to: Biodiversity, Climate Change, Climate Change-Kyoto Protocol, Desertification, Hazardous Wastes, Law of the Sea, Ozone Layer Protection, Ship Pollution, Wetlands

signed, but not ratified: Environmental Modification, Marine Life Conservation

Geography - note:

Nahr el Litani is the only major river in Near East not crossing an international boundary; rugged terrain historically helped isolate, protect, and develop numerous factional groups based on religion, clan, and ethnicity

Chapter 3: People and Society

Nationality:

noun: Lebanese (singular and plural)

adjective: Lebanese

Ethnic groups:

Arab 95%, Armenian 4%, other 1%

note: many Christian Lebanese do not identify themselves as Arab but rather as descendents of the ancient Canaanites and prefer to be called Phoenicians

Languages:

Arabic (official), French, English, Armenian

Religions:

Muslim 59.7% (Shia, Sunni, Druze, Isma'ilite, Alawite or Nusayri), Christian 39% (Maronite Catholic, Greek Orthodox, Melkite Catholic, Armenian Orthodox, Syrian Catholic, Armenian Catholic, Syrian Orthodox, Roman Catholic, Chaldean, Assyrian, Coptic, Protestant), other 1.3%

note: 17 religious sects recognized

Population:

4,131,583 (July 2013 est.)

country comparison to the world: 126

Age structure:

0-14 years: 22.1% (male 467,416/female 445,352)

15-24 years: 17.5% (male 368,097/female 353,518)

25-54 years: 42.4% (male 844,217/female 906,795)

55-64 years: 8.7% (male 165,271/female 193,312)

65 years and over: 9.4% (male 178,080/female

209,525) (2013 est.)

Median age:

total: 30.9 years

male: 29.7 years

female: 32.1 years (2013 est.)

Population growth rate:

-0.04% (2013 est.)

country comparison to the world: 201

Birth rate:

14.79 births/1,000 population (2013 est.)

country comparison to the world: 135

Death rate:

6.73 deaths/1,000 population (2013 est.)

country comparison to the world: 140

Net migration rate:

-8.48 migrant(s)/1,000 population (2013 est.)

country comparison to the world: 204

Urbanization:

urban population: 87.2% of total population (2011)

rate of urbanization: 0.86% annual rate of change (2010-15 est.)

Major urban areas - population:

BEIRUT (capital) 1.909 million (2009)

Sex ratio:

at birth: 1.05 male(s)/female

0-14 years: 1.05 male(s)/female

15-24 years: 1.04 male(s)/female

25-54 years: 0.93 male(s)/female

55-64 years: 0.86 male(s)/female

65 years and over: 0.86 male(s)/female

total population: 0.96 male(s)/female (2013 est.)

Maternal mortality rate:

25 deaths/100,000 live births (2010)

country comparison to the world: 130

Infant mortality rate:

total: 14.81 deaths/1,000 live births

country comparison to the world: 113

male: 14.98 deaths/1,000 live births

female: 14.64 deaths/1,000 live births (2013 est.)

Life expectancy at birth:

total population: 75.46 years

country comparison to the world: 94

male: 73.86 years

female: 77.13 years (2013 est.)

Total fertility rate:

1.75 children born/woman (2013 est.)

country comparison to the world: 164

Contraceptive prevalence rate:

58% (2004)

Health expenditures:

7% of GDP (2010)

country comparison to the world: 81

Physicians density:

3.54 physicians/1,000 population (2009)

Hospital bed density:

3.5 beds/1,000 population (2009)

Drinking water source:

improved:

urban: 100% of population

rural: 100% of population

total: 100% of population (2010 est.)

Sanitation facility access:

improved:

urban: 100% of population

rural: 87% of population

total: 98% of population

unimproved:

urban: 0% of population

rural: 13% of population

total: 2% of population (2000 est.)

HIV/AIDS - adult prevalence rate:

0.1% (2009 est.)

country comparison to the world: 144

HIV/AIDS - people living with HIV/AIDS:

3,600 (2009 est.)

country comparison to the world: 125

HIV/AIDS - deaths:

fewer than 500 (2009 est.)

country comparison to the world: 87

Obesity - adult prevalence rate:

27.4% (2008)

country comparison to the world: 40

Children under the age of 5 years underweight:

4.2% (2004)

country comparison to the world: 96

Education expenditures:

1.7% of GDP (2011)

country comparison to the world: 167

Literacy:

definition: age 15 and over can read and write

total population: 87.4%

male: 93.1%

female: 82.2% (2003 est.)

School life expectancy (primary to tertiary education):

total: 14 years

male: 14 years

female: 15 years (2011)

Child labor - children ages 5-14:

total number: 54,387

percentage: 7 % (2000 est.)

Unemployment, youth ages 15-24:

total: 22.1%

country comparison to the world: 51

male: 22.3%

female: 21.5% (2007)

Chapter 4: Government and Key Leaders

Country name:

conventional long form: Lebanese Republic

conventional short form: Lebanon

local long form: Al Jumhuriyah al Lubnaniyah

local short form: Lubnan

former: Greater Lebanon

Government type:

republic

Capital:

name: Beirut

geographic coordinates: 33 52 N, 35 30 E

time difference: UTC+2 (7 hours ahead of Washington, DC during Standard Time)

daylight saving time: +1hr, begins last Sunday in March; ends last Sunday in October

Administrative divisions:

6 governorates (mohafazat, singular - mohafazah); Beqaa, Beyrouth (Beirut), Liban-Nord, Liban-Sud, Mont-Liban, Nabatiye

note: two new governorates - Aakkar and Baalbek-Hermel - have been legislated but not yet implemented

Independence:

22 November 1943 (from League of Nations mandate under French administration)

National holiday:

Independence Day, 22 November (1943)

Constitution:

23 May 1926; amended a number of times, most recently in 1990 to include changes necessitated by the Charter of Lebanese National Reconciliation (Ta'if Accord) of October 1989

Legal system:

mixed legal system of civil law based on the French civil code, Ottoman legal tradition, and religious laws covering personal status, marriage, divorce, and other family relations of the Jewish, Islamic, and Christian communities

International law organization participation:

has not submitted an ICJ jurisdiction declaration; non-party state to the ICCt

Suffrage:

21 years of age; compulsory for all males; authorized for women at age 21 with elementary education; excludes military personnel

Executive branch:

<u>note</u>: following the resignation of Prime Minister Najib MIQATI and his Cabinet on 22 March 2013, the government is in caretaker status until a new prime minister is named and a new cabinet is formed

<u>chief of state</u>: President Michel SULAYMAN (since 25 May 2008)

<u>head of government</u>: Prime Minister Najib MIQATI (since 7 July 2011), Deputy Prime Minister Samir MOQBIL (since 7 July 2011)

<u>cabinet</u>: Cabinet chosen by the prime minister in consultation with the president and members of the National Assembly

<u>elections</u>: president elected by the National Assembly for a six-year term (may not serve consecutive terms); election last held on 25 May 2008 (next to be held in 2014); the prime minister and deputy prime minister appointed by the president in consultation with the National Assembly

<u>election results</u>: Michel SULAYMAN elected president; National Assembly vote - 118 for, 6 abstentions, 3 invalidated; 1 seat unfilled due to death of incumbent

Legislative branch:

unicameral National Assembly or Majlis al-Nuwab
(Arabic) or Assemblee Nationale (French) (128 seats;
members elected by popular vote on the basis of
sectarian proportional representation to serve four-
year terms)

elections: last held on 7 June 2009 (next to be held in
2013)

election results: percent of vote by group - March 8
Coalition 54.7%, March 14 Coalition 45.3%; seats by
group - March 14 Coalition 71; March 8 Coalition 57;
seats by party following 16 July 2012 byelection held
to fill one seat - March 14 Coalition 72, March 8
Coalition 56

Judicial branch:

highest court(s): Court of Cassation or Supreme Court
(organized into 4 divisions, each with a presiding
judge and 2 associate judges); Constitutional Council
(consists of 10 members)

judge selection and term of office: Court of Cassation
judges appointed by Supreme Judicial Council,
headed by the chief justice, and includes other
judicial officials; judge tenure NA; Constitutional
Council members appointed - 5 by the Council of

Ministers and 5 by parliament; members serve 5-year terms

subordinate courts: Courts of Appeal (6); Courts of First Instance; specialized tribunals, religious courts; military courts

Political parties and leaders:

14 March Coalition:

Democratic Left [Ilyas ATALLAH]

Democratic Renewal Movement [Nassib LAHUD]

Future Movement Bloc [Sa'ad al-HARIRI]

Kataeb Party [Amine GEMAYEL]

Lebanese Forces [Samir JA'JA]

Tripoli Independent Bloc

8 March Coalition:

Development and Resistance Bloc [Nabih BERRI, leader of Amal Movement]

Free Patriotic Movement [Michel AWN]

Loyalty to the Resistance Bloc [Mohammad RA'AD] (includes Hizballah [Hassan NASRALLAH])

Nasserite Popular Movement [Usama SAAD]

Popular Bloc [Elias SKAFF]

Syrian Ba'th Party [Sayez SHUKR]

Syrian Social Nationalist Party [Ali QANSO]

Tashnaq [Hovig MEKHITIRIAN]

Independent:

Democratic Gathering Bloc [Walid JUNBLATT, leader of Progressive Socialist Party]

Metn Bloc [Michel MURR]

Political pressure groups and leaders:

Maronite Church [Patriarch Bishara al-Ra'i]

other: note - most sects retain militias and a number of militant groups operate in Palestinian refugee camps

International organization participation:

ABEDA, AFESD, AMF, CAEU, FAO, G-24, G-77, IAEA, IBRD, ICAO, ICC (national committees), ICRM, IDA, IDB, IFAD, IFC, IFRCS, ILO, IMF, IMO, IMSO, Interpol, IOC, IPU, ISO, ITSO, ITU, LAS, MIGA, NAM, OAS (observer), OIC, OIF, OPCW, PCA, UN, UNCTAD, UNESCO, UNHCR, UNIDO, UNRWA, UNWTO, UPU, WCO, WFTU (NGOs), WHO, WIPO, WMO, WTO (observer)

Diplomatic representation in the US:

chief of mission: Ambassador Antoine CHEDID

chancery: 2560 28th Street NW, Washington, DC
20008

telephone: [1] (202) 939-6300

FAX: [1] (202) 939-6324

consulate(s) general: Detroit, New York, Los Angeles

Diplomatic representation from the US:

chief of mission: Ambassador Maura CONNELLY

embassy: Awkar, Lebanon (Awkar facing the
Municipality)

mailing address: P. O. Box 70-840, Antelias,
Lebanon; from US: US Embassy Beirut, 6070 Beirut
Place, Washington, DC 20521-6070

telephone: [961] (4) 542600, 543600

FAX: [961] (4) 544136

Key Leaders:

Pres.	Michel SULAYMAN
Prime Min.	Najib MIQATI
Dep. Prime Min.	Samir MOQBIL
Min. of Admin. Reform	Muhammad FNAYSH
Min. of Agriculture	Husayn al-Hajj HASSAN
Min. of Culture	Gabi LAYYOUN
Min. of Defense	Fayiz GHOSN

Min. of Displaced People	**Ala al-Din TERRO**
Min. of Economy & Trade	**Nicolas NAHHAS**
Min. of Education	**Hassan DIAB**
Min. of Energy & Water	**Gibran BASSIL**
Min. of Environment	**Nazim al-KHOURY**
Min. of Finance	**Muhammad SAFADI**
Min. of Foreign Affairs & Emigrants	**Adnan MANSOUR**
Min. of Industry	**Freij SABOUNJIAN**
Min. of Information	**Walid DAOUQ**
Min. of Interior	**Marwan CHARBEL**
Min. of Justice	**Shakib QORTABAWI**
Min. of Labor	**Charbel NAHHAS**
Min. of Public Health	**Ali Hassan KHALIL**
Min. of Social Affairs	**Wael Abu FAOUR**
Min. of Telecommunications	**Nicolas SAHNAWI**
Min. of Tourism	**Fady ABBOUD**
Min. of Transport & Public Works	**Ghazi ARIDI**
Min. of Youth & Sports	**Faysal KARAMI**
Min. of State	**Salim KARAM**
Min. of State	**Ahmad KARAMI**

Min. of State	**Marwan KHAYREDDINE**
Min. of State	**Panos MANIJIAN**
Min. of State	**Ali QANSO**
Min. of State for Parliamentary Affairs	**Nicolas FATTOUSH**
Governor, Central Bank of Lebanon	**Riad Toufic SALAMEH**
Ambassador to the US	**Antoine CHEDID**
Permanent Representative to the UN, New York	**Nawaf SALAM**

Flag description:

three horizontal bands consisting of red (top), white (middle, double width), and red (bottom) with a green cedar tree centered in the white band; the red bands symbolize blood shed for liberation, the white band denotes peace, the snow of the mountains, and purity; the green cedar tree is the symbol of Lebanon and represents eternity, steadiness, happiness, and prosperity

National symbol(s):

cedar tree

National anthem:

name: "Kulluna lil-watan" (All Of Us, For Our Country!)

lyrics/music: Rachid NAKHLE/Wadih SABRA

note: adopted 1927; the anthem was chosen following a nationwide competition

Chapter 5: Economy

Economy - overview:

Lebanon has a free-market economy and a strong laissez-faire commercial tradition. The government does not restrict foreign investment; however, the investment climate suffers from red tape, corruption, arbitrary licensing decisions, complex customs procedures, high taxes, tariffs, and fees, archaic legislation, and weak intellectual property rights. The Lebanese economy is service-oriented; main growth sectors include banking and tourism. The 1975-90 civil war seriously damaged Lebanon's economic infrastructure, cut national output by half, and derailed Lebanon's position as a Middle Eastern entrepot and banking hub. Following the civil war, Lebanon rebuilt much of its war-torn physical and financial infrastructure by borrowing heavily - mostly from domestic banks - saddling the government with a huge debt burden. Pledges of economic and financial reforms made at separate international donor conferences during the 2000s have mostly gone unfulfilled, including those made during the Paris III Donor Conference in 2007 following the July 2006 war. The collapse of the government in early 2011 over its backing of the Special Tribunal for Lebanon and unrest in neighboring Syria slowed economic growth to the 1-2% range in 2011-12, after four years of 8% average growth. In September 2011 the Cabinet endorsed a bill that would provide $1.2 billion in funding to improve Lebanon"s downtrodden electricity sector, but fiscal limitations will test the government"s ability to invest in other areas, such as water.

GDP (purchasing power parity):

$64.22 billion (2012 est.)

country comparison to the world: 88

$63.27 billion (2011 est.)

$62.34 billion (2010 est.)

note: data are in 2012 US dollars

GDP (official exchange rate):

$41.35 billion (2012 est.)

GDP - real growth rate:

1.5% (2012 est.)

country comparison to the world: 146

1.5% (2011 est.)

7% (2010 est.)

GDP - per capita (PPP):

$16,000 (2012 est.)

country comparison to the world: 84

$16,000 (2011 est.)

$16,000 (2010 est.)

note: data are in 2012 US dollars

GDP - composition by sector:

agriculture: 4.6%

industry: 19.7%

services: 75.8% (2012 est.)

Labor force:

0

country comparison to the world: 233

note: in addition, there are as many as 1 million foreign workers (2007 est.)

Labor force - by occupation:

agriculture: NA%

industry: NA%

services: NA%

Unemployment rate:

NA%

Population below poverty line:

28% (1999 est.)

Household income or consumption by percentage share:

lowest 10%: NA%

highest 10%: NA%

Investment (gross fixed):

32.9% of GDP (2012 est.)

country comparison to the world: 10

Budget:

revenues: $9.396 billion

expenditures: $13.32 billion (2012 est.)

Taxes and other revenues:

22.7% of GDP (2012 est.)

country comparison to the world: 146

Budget surplus (+) or deficit (-):

-9.5% of GDP (2012 est.)

country comparison to the world: 200

Public debt:

127.5% of GDP (2012 est.)

country comparison to the world: 6

133.2% of GDP (2011 est.)

note: data cover central government debt, and exclude debt instruments issued (or owned) by government entities other than the treasury; the data include treasury debt held by foreign entities; the data include debt issued by subnational entities, as well as intra-governmental debt; intra-governmental debt consists of treasury borrowings from surpluses in the social

funds, such as for retirement, medical care, and
unemployment

Inflation rate (consumer prices):

6.4% (2012 est.)

country comparison to the world: 169

5.1% (2011 est.)

Central bank discount rate:

3.5% (31 December 2010 est.)

country comparison to the world: 26

10% (31 December 2009 est.)

Commercial bank prime lending rate:

7.25% (31 December 2012 est.)

country comparison to the world: 120

7.53% (31 December 2011 est.)

Stock of narrow money:

$4.712 billion (31 December 2012 est.)

country comparison to the world: 101

$4.072 billion (31 December 2011 est.)

Stock of broad money:

$97.04 billion (31 December 2011 est.)

country comparison to the world: 56

$92 billion (31 December 2010 est.)

Stock of domestic credit:

$75.76 billion (31 December 2012 est.)

country comparison to the world: 60

$69.65 billion (31 December 2011 est.)

Market value of publicly traded shares:

$10.16 billion (31 December 2011)

country comparison to the world: 68

$12.59 billion (31 December 2010)

$12.89 billion (31 December 2009)

Agriculture - products:

citrus, grapes, tomatoes, apples, vegetables, potatoes, olives, tobacco; sheep, goats

Industries:

banking, tourism, food processing, wine, jewelry, cement, textiles, mineral and chemical products, wood and furniture products, oil refining, metal fabricating

Industrial production growth rate:

2.1% (2012 est.)

country comparison to the world: 96

Current account balance:

-$7.85 billion (2012 est.)

country comparison to the world: 172

-$4.163 billion (2011 est.)

Exports:

$5.662 billion (2012 est.)

$5.386 billion (2011 est.)

Exports - commodities:

jewelry, base metals, chemicals, miscellaneous consumer goods, fruit and vegetables, tobacco, construction minerals, electric power machinery and switchgear, textile fibers, paper

Exports - partners:

South Africa 16.9%, Switzerland 10.7%, UAE 8.7%, Saudi Arabia 8.5%, Syria 6.4%, Iraq 4.4% (2012)

Imports:

$20.38 billion (2012 est.)

country comparison to the world: 75

$19.3 billion (2011 est.)

Imports - commodities:

petroleum products, cars, medicinal products, clothing, meat and live animals, consumer goods, paper, textile fabrics, tobacco, electrical machinery and equipment, chemicals

Imports - partners:

US 11.2%, China 8.3%, Italy 7.8%, France 7.4%, Germany 5.4%, Turkey 4.7%, Egypt 4.1%, Greece 4.1% (2012)

Reserves of foreign exchange and gold:

$52.5 billion (31 December 2012 est.)

country comparison to the world: 34

$48.14 billion (31 December 2011 est.)

Debt - external:

$29.02 billion (31 December 2012 est.)

country comparison to the world: 73

$24.88 billion (31 December 2011 est.)

Stock of direct foreign investment - at home:

$NA

Stock of direct foreign investment - abroad:

$NA

Exchange rates:

Lebanese pounds (LBP) per US dollar:

1,507.5 (2012 est.)

1,507.5 (2011 est.)

1,507.5 (2010 est.)

1,507.5 (2009)

1,507.5 (2008)

Fiscal year:

calendar year

Chapter 6: Energy

Electricity - production:

12.98 billion kWh (2009 est.)

country comparison to the world: 88

Electricity - consumption:

12.34 billion kWh (2009 est.)

country comparison to the world: 84

Electricity - exports:

0 kWh (2010 est.)

country comparison to the world: 91

Electricity - imports:

1.155 billion kWh (2009 est.)

country comparison to the world: 61

Electricity - installed generating capacity:

2.314 million kW (2009 est.)

country comparison to the world: 98

Electricity - from fossil fuels:

87.9% of total installed capacity (2009 est.)

country comparison to the world: 81

Electricity - from nuclear fuels:

0% of total installed capacity (2009 est.)

country comparison to the world: 124

Electricity - from hydroelectric plants:

12.1% of total installed capacity (2009 est.)

country comparison to the world: 110

Electricity - from other renewable sources:

0% of total installed capacity (2009 est.)

country comparison to the world: 148

Crude oil - production:

0 bbl/day (2011 est.)

country comparison to the world: 154

Crude oil - exports:

0 bbl/day (2009 est.)

country comparison to the world: 140

Crude oil - imports:

0 bbl/day (2009 est.)

country comparison to the world: 206

Crude oil - proved reserves:

0 bbl (1 January 2012 est.)

country comparison to the world: 153

Refined petroleum products - production:

0 bbl/day (2008 est.)

country comparison to the world: 164

Refined petroleum products - consumption:

106,700 bbl/day (2011 est.)

country comparison to the world: 77

Refined petroleum products - exports:

0 bbl/day (2008 est.)

country comparison to the world: 192

Refined petroleum products - imports:

102,300 bbl/day (2008 est.)

country comparison to the world: 49

Natural gas - production:

0 cu m (2010 est.)

country comparison to the world: 152

Natural gas - consumption:

0 cu m (2010 est.)

country comparison to the world: 163

Natural gas - exports:

0 cu m (2010 est.)

country comparison to the world: 131

Natural gas - imports:

0 cu m (2010 est.)

country comparison to the world: 88

Natural gas - proved reserves:

0 cu m (1 January 2012 est.)

country comparison to the world: 156

Carbon dioxide emissions from consumption of energy:

15.24 million Mt (2010 est.)

country comparison to the world: 90

Chapter 7: Communications

Telephones - main lines in use:

900,000 (2011)

country comparison to the world: 82

Telephones - mobile cellular:

3.35 million (2011)

country comparison to the world: 121

Telephone system:

general assessment: repair of the telecommunications system, severely damaged during the civil war, now complete

domestic: two mobile-cellular networks provide good service; combined fixed-line and mobile-cellular subscribership roughly 100 per 100 persons

international: country code - 961; submarine cable links to Cyprus, Egypt, and Syria; satellite earth stations - 2 Intelsat (1 Indian Ocean and 1 Atlantic Ocean); coaxial cable to Syria (2011)

Broadcast media:

7 TV stations, 1 of which is state-owned; more than 30 radio stations, 1 of which is state-owned; satellite and cable TV services available; transmissions of at

least 2 international broadcasters are accessible through partner stations (2007)

Internet country code:

.lb

Internet hosts:

64,926 (2012)

country comparison to the world: 91

Internet users:

1 million (2009)

country comparison to the world: 99

Chapter 8: Transportation

Airports:

7 (2012)

country comparison to the world: 169

Airports - with paved runways:

total: 5

over 3,047 m: 1

2,438 to 3,047 m: 2

1,524 to 2,437 m: 1

under 914 m: 1 (2012)

Airports - with unpaved runways:

total: 2

914 to 1,523 m: 2 (2012)

Pipelines:

gas 88 km (2013)

Railways:

total: 401 km

country comparison to the world: 116

standard gauge: 319 km 1.435-m gauge

narrow gauge: 82 km 1.050-m gauge

note: rail system unusable because of the damage
done during fighting in the 1980s and in 2006 (2008)

Roadways:

<u>total</u>: 6,970 km (includes 170 km of expressways) (2005)

<u>country comparison to the world</u>: 148

Merchant marine:

<u>total</u>: 29

<u>country comparison to the world</u>: 85

<u>by type</u>: bulk carrier 4, cargo 7, carrier 17, vehicle carrier 1

<u>foreign-owned</u>: 2 (Syria 2)

<u>registered in other countries</u>: 34 (Barbados 2, Cambodia 5, Comoros 2, Egypt 1, Georgia 1, Honduras 2, Liberia 1, Malta 6, Moldova 1, Panama 2, Saint Vincent and the Grenadines 2, Sierra Leone 2, Togo 6, unknown 1) (2010)

Ports and terminals:

Beirut, Tripoli

Chapter 9: Military

Military branches:

Lebanese Armed Forces (LAF): Lebanese Army ((Al Jaysh al Lubnani) includes Lebanese Navy (Al Quwwat al Bahiriyya al Lubnaniya), Lebanese Air Force (Al Quwwat al Jawwiya al Lubnaniya)) (2013)

Military service age and obligation:

17-30 years of age for voluntary military service; 18-24 years of age for officer candidates; no conscription (2013)

Manpower available for military service:

males age 16-49: 1,081,016

females age 16-49: 1,115,349 (2010 est.)

Manpower fit for military service:

males age 16-49: 920,825

females age 16-49: 941,806 (2010 est.)

Manpower reaching militarily significant age annually:

male: 36,856

female: 35,121 (2010 est.)

Military expenditures:

2.5% of GDP (2012)

country comparison to the world: 55

Chapter 10: Transnational Issues

Disputes - international:

lacking a treaty or other documentation describing the boundary, portions of the Lebanon-Syria boundary are unclear with several sections in dispute; since 2000, Lebanon has claimed Shab'a Farms area in the Israeli-occupied Golan Heights; the roughly 2,000-strong UN Interim Force in Lebanon has been in place since 1978

Refugees and internally displaced persons:

refugees (country of origin): 436,154 (Palestinian refugees (UNRWA)); 8,751 (Iraq) (2011); 584,584 (Syria) (2013)

IDPs: at least 47,000 (1975-90 civil war, 2007 Lebanese security forces' destruction of Palestinian refugee camp) (2011)

Illicit drugs:

cannabis cultivation dramatically reduced to 2,500 hectares in 2002 despite continued significant cannabis consumption; opium poppy cultivation minimal; small amounts of Latin American cocaine and Southwest Asian heroin transit country on way to European markets and for Middle Eastern consumption; money laundering of drug proceeds fuels concern that extremists are benefiting from drug trafficking

Map of Lebanon

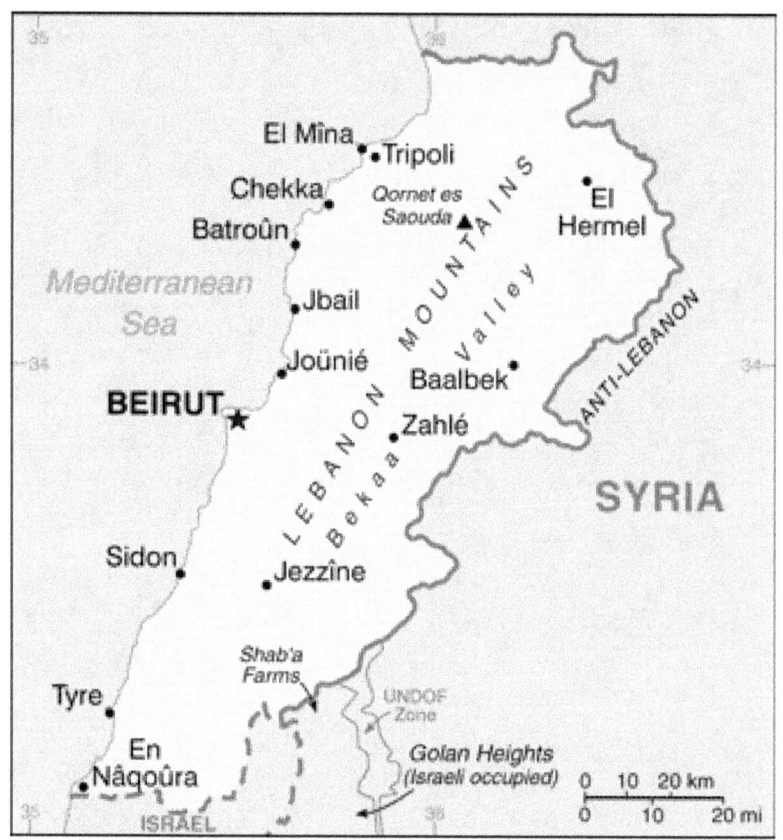

Other Key Facts™ Titles

Key Facts on Syria

Key Facts on China

Key Facts on Qatar

Key Facts on India

Key Facts on Germany

Key Facts on Argentina

Key Facts on Russia

Key Facts on North Korea

Key Facts on Brazil

Key Facts on Italy

Key Facts on the United Arab Emirates

Key Facts on the European Union

Key Facts on Pakistan

Key Facts on Saudi Arabia

Key Facts on Cyprus

Key Facts on Iran

Key Facts on Afghanistan

Key Facts on Iraq

Key Facts on Indonesia

Key Facts on South Korea

Key Facts on France

Key Facts on the United Kingdom

Key Facts on Egypt

Key Facts on Israel

Key Facts on Mexico

Key Facts on the United States of America

Key Facts on Turkey

Key Facts on South Africa

Key Facts on Greece

Key Facts on Japan

Key Facts on Malaysia

Key Facts on Vietnam

Key Facts on Hong Kong

Key Facts on Jordan

Key Facts on Australia

Key Facts on Venezuela

Key Facts on Canada

Key Facts on Burma (Myanmar)

Key Facts on Myanmar (Burma)

Key Facts on Singapore

Key Facts on Ireland

Key Facts on The Philippines

Key Facts on Thailand

Key Facts on Yemen

Key Facts on Bahrain

Key Facts on Kuwait

All Key Facts™ Titles are Available at

www.Amazon.com

THE INTERNATIONALIST®

2013

WWW.INTERNATIONALIST.COM